A Short Life of LUTHER

ALLAN W. TOWNSEND

FORTRESS PRESS
PHILADELPHIA

Library of Congress Catalog Card Number 67-21532

5572A67 Printed in U. S. A. 1-1006

ILLUSTRATIONS

The sources of the illustrations appearing in the text are gratefully acknowledged. Courtyard of birthplace in Eisleben, page 10, and The Cotta House at Eisenach, page 15, both by courtesy of Lutherhalle, Wittenberg; Luther the Preacher, from a painting by Lucas Cranach the Elder, courtesy of Gunther Beyer, Weimar, page 27; 95 Theses, by Paul Remmey, © Fortress Press, page 32; The Diet at Worms, by Paul Remmey, © Fortress Press, page 46; Table Talk, by James Schucker, © Fortress Press, page 58; Luther's manuscript of Psalm 43 from his translation of the Bible in the collection of Karl F. Reinking, Germany, page 62; Martin Luther, from a painting by Lucas Cranach the Elder in the National Museum, Stockholm, and Katherine von Bora, from a painting by Lucas Cranach the Elder in the National Museum at Berlin, pages 70 and 71.

TO MY FATHER AND MOTHER,
WITH GRATITUDE

FOREWORD

This little volume is intended for the general audience as an introduction to the life and thought of the sixteenth-century theologian, Martin Luther. It should be made clear that a more detailed biography would have to take into account a number of issues that are not herein discussed. The problems in Luther-interpretation are multitudinous. The distinction between legend and fact in Luther's early years, the dating of his "evangelical discovery," and a host of other matters are still open to debate among Luther scholars. The reader should be aware that these difficulties exist, although treatment of them is outside the scope of this brief sketch.

I wish to acknowledge my indebtedness to my teacher and friend, Professor B. A. Gerrish, of the University of Chicago. His inspiration and scholarly insight have been of inestimable help. Any shortcomings in this volume, however, are strictly the fault of the author.

ALLAN W. TOWNSEND

McCormick Theological Seminary
Chicago, Illinois
February, 1967

CONTENTS

FOREWORD iii

DEATH AT SIXTY-THREE

The Journey Home 1
His Last Good Work 2
Final Tributes 3
Luther Today 5

WHO CAN SAY IF GOD WANTS ME?

Humble Beginnings 9
Luther's Education 13
The Terror of Death 18
The Quest for a Gracious God 19

THE HAPPY EXCHANGE

Servant of the Word 23
Discovery of the Gospel of God 27
The Indulgence Controversy 30
The Protest Against Rome 35

ENEMIES OF THE GOSPEL

The Message of Freedom 40
On Trial Before the World 44
Luther in Hiding 47
The Protest Against the Radical Reformers 50

GROWING PAINS

Social and Political Unrest 53
The Two Kingdoms 54
New Life in the Converted Cloister 57
The Emerging Church 61

DICTATOR OR PROPHET?

Voices of Dissent 65
The Sacrament Controversy 67
New Negotiations for Unity 68
The Old Man at Wittenberg 69

FOOTNOTES 76

DEATH AT SIXTY-THREE

"The summons of death comes to us all, and no one can die for another. . . . Therefore, every one must himself know and be armed with the chief things that concern a Christian."[1]

The Journey Home

Luther was dead. According to a friend, he had been dying for more than a year. He had thought about death, preached about death, conversed about death, written about death. Only a few days before he had remarked in his own earthy fashion, "God willing that I return to Wittenberg, I shall eat and drink heartily so the worms will have a good fat doctor of theology on which to feed." But he was not to return to Wittenberg—at least not alive. Luther died at Eisleben, the town of his birth, on the eighteenth of February, 1546. He was sixty-three years old.

A messenger was dispatched to Wittenberg with a full report of the circumstances of his dying. When John Frederick, the prince of the province in which Luther lived, heard the news, he requested that the body be returned to Wittenberg to be buried with distinction in the Castle Church. Thus began the long and mournful journey home.

An honor guard of some fifty horsemen accompanied the tin coffin that contained the body of the Reverend Doctor. Bells tolled all along the eighty miles from Eisleben to Wittenberg, and people from the villages and countryside came to witness the sad procession and to pay final tribute to this stormy figure who about a quarter of a century before had released a revolution that had cracked the spiritual and political foundations of the Western world.

His Last Good Work

Luther's reason for being in Eisleben, old and sick as he was, and in the midst of the winter season, is itself a tribute to the man. The Counts of Mansfeld, who ruled the land of Luther's childhood, were engaged in a bitter family quarrel. When the situation proved intolerable, they appealed to Luther for help. Aware of the shortness of his days, the tiresome wrangling that would be involved in the arbitration, and the danger of the inclement weather to his health, the aging Luther still consented to use his office and his person to bring about a reconciliation. With his two youngest sons, Martin and Paul, and other companions, he traveled to Eisleben where he was able to participate in the restoration of peace among the noble family and to give thanks to God for this manifestation of his grace. It was just after ending the dispute between the Counts of Mansfeld that Luther became ill for the last time.

Few deaths in the history of famous men have been recorded in such detail. Luther's colleagues, aware of the significance of the event, saw to it that several eyewitnesses were on hand to certify the closing moments of the Reformer's life. Their reports testify that he had heeded his own words and was truly well-armed for the death-struggle. In his last hours, he prayed fervently, commended his spirit to Almighty God, and held firmly to the bare promise from John's Gospel that "God so loved the world that he gave his only Son, that whoever believes in him should not perish but have eternal life" (John 3:16, *RSV*).

In Luther's day, much more so than in our own, death was regarded as a "moment of truth" and the death-style of a man the revelation of his true character. Wild inventions concerning the demise of controversial figures frequently sprang up from nowhere. False rumors of Luther's dying had been circulated even while he was yet alive, including one infamous Italian report that took great delight in depicting Luther's association with the Devil. Hence, his friend Justus Jonas, who had been with him at Eisleben, asked the sinking man in a loud voice, "Reverend Father, are you willing to die in the name of Christ and the doctrine which you have preached?" With a last burst of strength, Luther uttered, "Yes!"

Final Tributes

Word of Luther's death reached Philip Melanchthon the following day, February 19. Melanchthon, Luther's university colleague and his Right Arm in the cause of the Gospel, was scheduled to deliver his morning lectures on the Epistle to the Romans. Deeply moved by the loss, Melanchthon could only relate the news to his students, taking care that they received the correct details so that they would not be deceived by false reports. "The Charioteer and the Chariot of Israel is gone," Melanchthon told them, "he who guided the Church in these last days of the world. For assuredly this doctrine of forgiveness of sin and of trust in the Son of God was not invented by the wisdom of man, and we ourselves have seen that Luther was awakened by God."

Three days later, on the morning of February 22, Luther's funeral cortege arrived at the Elster Gate of Wittenberg, the same gate at which the young Luther, in righteous defiance, had burned to ashes the Holy Father's Bull of Excommunication. Now, the university faculty, with leading town officials and thousands of other citizens, joined the cortege in the final procession down the narrow street leading to the Castle Church. Following the knights and horsemen, in the carriage immediately behind the hearse, rode Luther's wife, Katherine. As they approached the town square, they were met by the student-body, led by the local pastor, Johannes Bugenhagen. From there they proceeded to the Castle Church, where the body was carried through the same door on which Luther, twenty-nine years before, had nailed the *Ninety-Five Theses*.

Two memorial services had already been held for Luther at Eisleben, with his friends Justus Jonas and Michael Coelius preaching.[2] Now it remained for Bugenhagen and Melanchthon to pay their final tributes. All of these theologians saw Luther as a man inspired by God, but it is perhaps Melanchthon's funeral oration, delivered from the side of Luther's coffin before the crowded church, that is the loftiest, and yet, most discriminating of the final testimonies.

Melanchthon tried to avoid a eulogy of Luther's person and instead spoke of Luther's relation to the church. In so doing, he included Luther in a long line of illustrious men chosen by God to gather and establish his people. Melanchthon told the mourning congregation that, much to the dismay and disorder of the Roman Church hierarchy, Luther had clarified the doctrine of repentance for the comfort of tormented consciences and anxious souls, expounding Paul's doctrine of ultimate acceptance through trust in Jesus Christ, who forgives while we are yet *unforgivable*. According to Melanchthon, Luther had shown the difference between the Two Kingdoms, the Rule of the Gospel and the Rule of the Law, delineating how the morality or righteousness of faith differs from that of civil morality. He had demonstrated that the *true* worship of God is a happy confidence and a good conscience in and through one mediator, Jesus, the Savior—a faith that flows forth in love and joy for one's fellow man.

Melanchthon also proclaimed that by declaring the home and the job as the sphere for good works and the fulfillment of the Christian life, Luther had blessed the worldly occupations of man in a way that had not been done by any other spokesman for the church. And, said Melanchthon, he gave to the German people a translation of the Bible that was so lucid that it was more easily understood than most commentaries on the book!

As he continued, Melanchthon could not refrain from speaking of Luther in a more personal way. Quite aware of Luther's exhibitions of verbal violence and coarse abuse in his struggles with the Roman church authorities and the radical reformers who came in his wake, Melanchthon said, "I will not deny this. But I answer in the language of Erasmus: 'Because of the magnitude of the disorders, God gave this age a violent physician.' " There was no denying that Luther was an ardent man, but, said Melanchthon, those who knew him closely knew him to be a kind and affectionate person, desirous of peace, and not a factious spirit. His severity resulted from his zeal for the truth, not from personal malice.

Luther Today

How shall we evaluate the man Luther, his life, and work? He has been called an irrationalist, a libertine, a Jew-hater, a rebellious spirit, the father of Individualism, a colossal crybaby. He has been accredited with being the spiritual ancestor of Adolph Hitler and the champion of Jesus Christ. Because he wrote so much, over such a long period of time, out of so many different situations, and in so many varied moods, it is possible to make Luther say nearly anything one wishes.

We might, however, in making our own historical assessment, take a clue from Luther himself, who had little patience for the academics of his day that tiptoed through the writings of the fathers as though every dropping from their pen was a word of doctrine. He once remarked that he hoped when he was dead people would not make the same mistake with his writings—that they would realize that he, like the fathers, had had to fight many issues which would no longer be comprehensible to following generations. One had to learn to *read*, Luther said, to discern the word of truth, and to forgive, forget, and give up to history much of what had been uttered. This is especially true of Luther, who often used his writing as an emotional catharsis. He was a passionate spirit, whose temperament was always in his writings, whose heart was always in his words. He was no speculative theologian, writing of God and man once removed from the heat of life. And, just because of the visceral character of his work, emerging from varied existential predicaments, he often appears self-contradictory. Yet, the open reader finds in Luther motifs that run throughout everything he did and said, consistent concerns that are not dated by milieu and from which we can derive an appreciation of his contributions in the saving history of God.

Luther, the man, was truly a saint—not in the ordinary sense of the word, but in the *biblical* sense. That is, he was one who sought his goodness in the mercy of Christ rather than in his own moral achievements. He himself remarked that to live as Titus 2:12 says, "soberly, righteously, and godly, in this present world," is like keeping sober in a tavern, chaste in a whorehouse, godly in a dance hall, and guiltless in the midst of thieves and murderers. This is not to say that Luther was licentious or full of uncontrollable appetites. He could be as well-disciplined as the most austere of "saints." But, in his profound understanding of the nature of sin, he knew that to be a man in this fallen world was to participate in the fruits of unbelief and pride. His ethical motivation came not from any inherent goodness that he might have possessed (he didn't believe he possessed any), but from the power of Christ's promise to him that he was forgiven and accepted into God's presence out of the abundance of *God's mercy*. It was this internal renewal, created by the Word of God, that issued forth in works of charity and love—a foreign righteousness created by a word from the outside. And it was in the hope of *God's* righteousness that he abided.

It is interesting to note that for Luther the definition of a Christian was not a "holier-than-thou" person, or one who "every day and in every way is getting better and better." For him, maturing in the Christian faith meant fleeing more and more to the mercy of Christ and the forgiveness of sin. This was his "Spiritual Revolution." Man's salvation rests not on man's decision for God, but on God's decision for man. And, according to Luther, God has decided for us. Christ has died *for me*. This realization broke upon Luther in all its fullness and he felt as though the gates of paradise had opened. Paradoxically, it was this joy in the Lord that led him into spiritual war with Rome.

To be accurate, one must speak of the sixteenth century not as the Age of Reformation, but as a period of reformations. Luther and the Evangelicals were but one of several reform groups concerned with the course of the church. Whatever else the other movements might have been, Luther's reformation was first of all the rediscovery of the Gospel—that gracious invitation of God to stand in his presence without reasons in our hands—and the proclamation of this gospel of free forgiveness for the sake of frightened, distraught, and emotionally tormented people. Luther's cause was and remained throughout his lifetime essentially a *pastoral* cause.

Religion had become a political and commercial enterprise. A debased system of indulgences, exaggerated relic devotion, the pilgrimage fad, idolatry of the saints—all these things catered to people's guilt and superstition and were popular means by which ambitious church and civil officials raised funds. Against these outward abuses, and the inner spirit that gave rise to them, was juxtaposed Luther's discovery of God's *unqualified* forgiveness, a declaration that again made it possible for sinners to relate to God without all the trappings of a religious-ethical system carefully designed to appease the Deity and to assuage man's fear of the Holy.

Luther's reformation, however, was more than a rediscovery of the Gospel. The Roman Church, even at the height of its arrogance, had not been without the Gospel. But Luther reestablished the Gospel as *the sole interpretive principle* of Christian faith and practice. The constellation of meaning that formed in Luther's person and work brought about the rediscovery of what it means to live by grace through faith in the forgiveness of sin with such insight and depth that it can only be said that it had never been understood so clearly before, not even in most of the apostolic writings. The Gospel of Christ was born again in all its original power, and this Gospel, in Luther's reformation at any rate, was again to become the key for understanding not only the Bible, but all theological thought and religious practice. All glory was given to God alone. "If any man boast, let him boast in the Lord." In this conviction, Luther remained steadfast till his death.

WHO CAN SAY IF GOD WANTS ME?

"If God abandons our hearts, so that we lose all sense of confidence, then we are faced by blank despair; for whether or not we actually know sin in our hearts, we flounder on one thought: who can say if God wants me?"[3]

Humble Beginnings

Martin Luther's father would have been pleased to know of Luthers' role as mediator in the dispute between the Counts of Mansfeld. Hans Luther had once had his heart set on Martin's becoming a lawyer and had dreamed of the days when his lawyer-son would assume a position of prominence in the courts of the Mansfeld princes. Like so many parents who hope to better themselves through their children, Hans was greatly disappointed. His bitterness over Martin's disobedience in the choice of vocation was not easily abated. That Luther's personal history should have ended with his serving the princely family in a capacity quite above that of Hans's expectation most certainly would have been a source of satisfaction to the old man.

Hans Luther was a German peasant. His family was not of the lowest economic order. They owned land. But their life was tough and their worldly assets meager. Since Hans was not in line to inherit the family farm and law did not permit the division of peasant property (the youngest got all, leaving the older sons to shift for themselves), he turned to copper

mining. The Moehra region in which he grew up was just awakening to the mining industry, and it was here that Hans got his start.

He married a girl named Margarete Ziegler who belonged to a respected family in the neighboring region of Eisenach. It was not long after their marriage that Hans, pursuing his responsibilities as provider, moved with his young wife a hundred miles to the northeast to Eisleben, a town thriving on the industry from the copper mines in the county of Mansfeld.

Just how long the Luthers were in Eisleben before the birth of Martin is not known, but tradition has fixed the date of his birth on the tenth of November, 1483. The following day his parents presented him for baptism in the Tower Chapel of St. Peter's Church, where he was named for the calendar saint of that day, St. Martin of Tours, founder of French monasticism. Martin was the first of several children born to Hans and Margarete.

In the spring of 1484, the family moved again, this time to Mansfeld, a town closer to the Hartz mountains and more the center of the mining region. It was in the Mansfeld region that Luther was to grow into adolescence. Mansfeld was beautiful country, characterized by hills, meadows, woods, and plains, and overlooked by the majestic castle of the Counts of Mansfeld that jutted upward from its foundation atop a steep cliff.

Though Luther grew up in this pastoral setting, his own childhood was far from idyllic. There was not an overabundance of affection in the Luther household. Hans and Margarete, members of the rising middle class, struggled hard to improve their worldly position and their preoccupation with this enterprise, along with their firm belief in unquestioned parental authority, left little room for the carefree frolics and often unruly wills of growing children. Their discipline was not always in the best interest of the child. Luther recalled that on account of his having taken a single nut without permission, his mother had beaten him until the blood flowed. He also mentioned that there had been times when his father had so alienated him through severe punishment that the elder Luther had to go to great pains to regain Martin's loyalty and affection. While this strict rule was not altogether uncommon in that day, on more than one occasion Luther attributed his entering the monastery to such abuses. "Where such fear enters a man," he said, "it can hardly be rooted out again as long as he lives. As he once trembled at every word of his father and mother, to the end of his life he is afraid of a rustling leaf."[4]

Despite the severity of his early training, Luther respected his parents throughout his lifetime. He often took pride in the fact that he came from peasant stock, though he was quick to point out that boasting of one's ancestry made about as much sense as the Devil's priding himself on his angelic lineage! Hans Luther could be a jovial father on occasion, kind and affectionate toward his children. And Luther's mother, full as she was of the crippling superstition and folklore of the times –she was for a while convinced that a neighbor was a witch who had put a spell on the Luther household–carried out her motherly duties in a faithful manner. She sang to her children, and from her Luther learned such humble wisdom as:

> If folk don't like you and me
> The fault with us is like to be.

From his father, Luther seemed to inherit even more of the practical values typified in the best of the sturdy, industrious peasant people. Tradition has it that Hans, when he once lay critically ill, was told by a priest to give his money to the church and thereby make his peace with God. Hans, however, replied that he would give his money to his children because they needed it more. This practical strain in Hans that took affront at the idea of having to pay the clergy at the neglect of the common life in order to appease God, was to find fuller expression in the mature theology of Luther, who, as Melanchthon stated in his funeral address, blessed the worldly life of man as it had not been blessed by any theologian before.

Luther's Education

If Luther's home life was difficult, his days at school were even more so. Physical punishment and personal humiliation were the chief means for maintaining order and insuring that the students did their schoolwork. At the Mansfeld Latin School, to which Luther was packed off at an age so young that he had to be carried on the shoulders of an older friend, the teacher kept a slate at the front of the room on which names were recorded for academic mistakes and acts of misbehavior. At the end of the week, punishment was meted out—a wallop on the bottomside for each time one's name appeared on the slate. Luther recalled that he received as many as fifteen strokes on one morning. The sting of these experiences never left him. He remembered his early schooling as "purgatory and hell." And in his mature years, he became a leading advocate for educational reform, asserting among other things that the apple must always accompany the rod.

At the Mansfeld school, Luther learned the ABC's of Latin, the Western world's liturgical and scholarly language, and memorized prayers and portions of the Latin Bible, received instruction in music, and had practice in Rhetoric, which included the learning of proper forms and styles of communication and the reading of literature. While the Mansfeld Latin School might not have rated very highly by later humanistic standards, it provided Luther with a good enough background to enable him to meet the demands of more advanced training without serious difficulty. And even though he was severely critical of the harsh treatment at the hands of the teachers, these early experiences never seemed to have diminished his eager quest for new knowledge—a quality that Melanchthon, again in Luther's funeral oration, said stayed with Luther all of his days.

Luther showed great promise as a student, and Hans was anxious to see his son climb the ladder of success. His worldly position having prospered enough that he could release Martin from his obligation of staying home to help with the family mining business, Hans sent his fourteen-year-old son to school at Magdeburg. It is generally believed that here Luther came under the teachings of the Brethren of the Common Life, an order devoted to the renewal of simple piety and the regular reading of the Scriptures for both clergy and laity.

Because of the large number of churches and chapels in Magdeburg and the great number of clergy required to attend the various altars, it was called a "miniature Rome." There were many impressive religious festivals and processions, all in stark contrast to the cadaverous Prince William of Anhalt, patron of the Franciscan monastery, who begged in the streets of Magdeburg, looking like a dead man because of his fasts and mortification of his body. "At the sight of him," Luther said, "no one could keep from being moved and ashamed of his own secular life."

Luther was in Magdeburg for only one year. He next went

to school in Eisenach, his mother's home region. There he came into contact with some excellent teachers, including an educator named Trebonious who, Luther said, tipped his scholar's cap upon entering the classroom in respect for his students who would eventually grow up to be distinguished citizens. This more favorable environment helped young Martin grow more rapidly.

Eisenach was the finishing school for Luther in more ways than just being the final academic preparation before his entering the university. Luther sang and begged with other students in the streets of Eisenach to help defray the expense of education. In the course of this activity he came into favor with Frau Cotta, wife of a rich businessman. Ursula Cotta was struck by Martin's singing and was fascinated by his eyes, a feature many were to be taken by as the years evolved. She took Luther into their household, and being a woman of some warmth and charm, gave Luther the affection of a mother's love and refinement in manners that would permit him to mingle at ease with people from all walks of life. The Cottas proved a "second family" for Luther, and in return he tutored the children. From Frau Cotta he learned the proverb, "There is no greater gift on earth than a woman's gift of love to her husband." All in all, it was a very positive experience for Luther and he remembered his stay in Eisenach as one of the happiest periods in his life.

In the spring of 1501, Luther entered the University of Erfurt. Erfurt numbered around two thousand students, and had an excellent academic reputation. In his first year of study, he did not stand out particularly–he was thirtieth in a class of fifty-seven. But in 1505, when he received the Master's degree, he ranked second in a class of seventeen

While at Erfurt, Luther kept company with a small circle of students called the "poets" who devoted themselves to the art of writing and gathered regularly to read and criticize one another's work. Luther's main interest, however, leaned more toward philosophy. His knowledge and skill in this field earned for him the title "The Philosopher" from his friends. The philosophical tradition to which he attached himself was called the New Way, after the teachings of William Ockham, a professor in Oxford. The Ockhamist school affirmed the usefulness of human reason in theology, but flatly denied reason's ability to prove demonstratively articles of faith such as the existence of God. The New Way was opposed to the system of thought represented in the tradition of Thomas Aquinas which asserted the value of human reason in finding truth even in matters of faith. The New Way objected to this "imperialism of reason" and fought its encroachment upon areas where they maintained only revelation can provide true knowledge. While Luther was later to call even the Ockhamists "hog-theologians," he retained some of their basic tenets and developed them further in his own thinking.

It was during his years at Erfurt that Luther also polished his musical abilities. This was brought about in part through a serious accident that befell him on his way home from the university. He tripped and severely cut his leg on the academic sword he was wearing. While a friend with whom he was traveling ran to get a doctor, Martin lay flat on his back with his leg in the air and pressed the wound with his hand to stop the bleeding. It was a long time before he recovered from this nearly fatal injury. While recuperating, he taught himself to play the lute, a guitar-type instrument which he mastered and enjoyed playing for the rest of his life. He came to be called "The Musician" by his friends in addition to "The Philosopher."

The Terror of Death

The Master's beret was bestowed upon Luther in 1505 and he was carried through the streets in a jubilant torchlight celebration honoring the newly donned scholars. His father was so proud that he no longer addressed Martin with the familiar "du," but with the polite, formal "Sie." And out of joy over Martin's success and progress, he bought him the expensive set of books, *Corpus Juris*, the perfect gift for his son as he continued his study of law at Erfurt.

Martin attended the lectures for two months. Then he returned home again. What transpired between him and his parents on that visit is not known. Luther was obviously not taken by the prospect of a career in law. Neither was he happy about the plans Hans was making for him to marry into a rich family. It could only have been a disappointing visit. On his way back to Erfurt through a thunderstorm, Luther was struck to the ground by a bolt of lightning, and in his terror cried out to St. Ann, patron saint of the miners, "Save me and I shall become a monk!"

Catholic historians are right in saying that Luther was not the type for monastic life, though this in no way takes away from his rigorous devotion to the monastic discipline—a discipline he maintained in part many years after he had been freed from his vows. His excellent intellectual and social development equipped him for a life of quite a different nature. Luther was driven into the monastery by a combination of forces beyond reason that led him to go against his parents, his friends, and above all, his own better judgment. His accident with the sword, the untimely death of a close friend, and all the formless fears that had appeared sporadically throughout his student days, now crystallized around the thunderstorm event, causing him to abandon the life-direction that had been set for him by his father and to begin in earnest his quest for a gracious God.

The milieu in which Luther lived was dominated by the great triumverate–Death, the Devil, and Hell. Christ was seen principally as the judge of the living and the dead, and the church as the one hope against eternal damnation, it having the salvational ways and means to insure the believer's being numbered among the children of paradise. Having been cut down on the threshold of manhood, his self-confidence utterly shaken, and the threat of death so dramatically impressed upon him, Luther fled further into the life of the church. There was no better way to appeal for divine favor than by pursuing a church vocation. Denial of certain worldly privileges was but a momentary sacrifice in comparison to the weight of glory in store for those who took God seriously and followed the steps of salvation offered by the medieval church.

Fourteen days after his terrifying experience on the road to Erfurt, Luther held a farewell party at which he drank and sang with his friends for the last time. His books, including the recently purchased volumes of *Corpus Juris* that Hans had so proudly given him, had been turned over to the bookseller, and the morning following the party, accompanied by sorrowing companions, Luther presented himself at the door of the Augustinian cloister.

The Quest for a Gracious God

Luther said that in entering the monastery he was "trying to get a gracious God." This may be somewhat misleading, however, for in actuality he seemed not so much trying to get a gracious God as he was trying to prove himself acceptable to the God he already had. In other words, this period of his life has as its motif the drive toward self-justification, an issue that became acute at the age of twenty-two.

Monastery regulations required a probationary period to test the sincerity of those desiring to take the road of self-denial. Martin was presented to the prior of the convent and then housed in a guest room of the cloister till the time in which the brothers should be convinced that his call was of God. Whether or not Hans Luther conferred with Martin during this probational period is not known, but at the news of his son's decision, Hans nearly went wild. He finally gave Martin his consent only after two of his other sons died in the plague that was then raging through the area (friends interpreted this as an act of judgment against Hans), and then he gave it only grudgingly.

With the heads of the cloister finally convinced that it was a legitimate call, Martin was received into the order as a novitiate at an impressive ceremony in which he prostrated himself before the assembly and declared his intention to surrender his self-will, mortify his flesh, accept the poverty, and attend the vigils—all the self-negating discipline demanded of those who would prove worthy of God. This was the beginning of a whole new life for Martin. Everything had to change. Only his name might remain the same. He was led from the chapel to his cell, a small six-by-nine cubicle with a single window, unheated through the long winter, and containing only the barest essentials in furnishings. Here it was that Martin would spend long hours in prayer, Bible reading, and mortification of his body. The Augustinian Observants were one of the strictest monastic orders and the physical and mental burden of the radically new life lay heavily on the novice. Yet Luther had the ability to adapt, and in these years he surpassed the physical requirements imposed by the order, often to the detriment of his physical and emotional health.

At the end of his probationary year in which he proved to his superiors the genuineness of his motivation and his suitability for the ascetic way of life, Luther was made a full brother of the order. The order comprised two distinct divisions, the clergy and the laity. Officers of the cloister, having recognized Luther's gifts, early designated him as a candidate for the priesthood. His preparation included the study of the exposition of the Mass by Gabriel Biel, and Luther was profoundly moved by the stirring description of the great mystery entrusted to the priests of God. By the spring of 1507 he was ordained a priest of the altar.

The celebration of his first Mass was a festive day for family and friends. Hans turned up with twenty horsemen and a very substantial gift of money. The first Mass was a moment of deep personal meaning for Luther. He almost fled from the altar during the service because of the dread that overtook him when, in the Mass, he addressed God Almighty without benefit of a mediator; but he was kept at his station by a preceptor and finished the celebration. Following the service, he received many congratulations, though Hans still was not fully reconciled to Martin's having chosen the religious life. At the reception, when Martin referred to the thunderstorm event as a call from heaven, Hans suggested that it might have been a delusion. And when someone expressed surprise that Hans should have been reluctant to give his blessing to Martin at the time he became a novice, Hans snapped back, "Don't you know that it is written, 'Thou shalt honor thy father and thy mother'?"

Luther entered into his new priestly duties with vigor.

There were many altars in the country around Erfurt served by the Augustinians and he took great pride in saying the Mass whenever he could. He later remarked that he had become a "slave" of the Mass, so much did he desire the benefits it bestowed upon those who performed it. In addition to his priestly duties, Luther had been selected as one having the makings of a professor and his superiors arranged for him to begin formal theological studies leading to the Doctor of Theology degree. He advanced rapidly in his theological training and in 1508 was called to the University of Wittenberg to lecture on moral philosophy and to offer survey courses in books of the Bible. In 1509 he was recalled to Erfurt to help in the lectures on Peter Lombard's *Sentences*, one of the standard theological works of the day. In 1510 he went to Rome on monastic business, and in 1511 he returned to Wittenberg where he was appointed preacher and, soon after, awarded the degree of Doctor of Theology.

While Luther's outward record was excellent during these five years of religious work and graduate study, inwardly there was a growing turmoil, and the awful fear that the monastic system, however rigorously obeyed, might not really be enough to insure salvation. How can a man really be sure after he's done all that is to be done that he still has done enough? Who can really be sure that God wants him? Christ was still for Luther like a flash of lightning and his insecurity before God deepened as he searched the Scriptures. He remained in terror of ultimate rejection, and hatred for God often flooded his heart.

THE HAPPY EXCHANGE

"The love of God which lives in man loves sinners . . . in order to make them righteous. . . . Rather than seeking its own good, the love of God flows forth and bestows good. Therefore sinners are attractive because they are loved; they are not loved because they are attractive. . . . This is the love of the cross. . . ."[5]

Servant of the Word

Luther's commitment to monastic discipline won him a trip to Rome. A plan of unification was in effect for the German Augustinian congregations, some of which had adopted earlier reform laws and others that had not responded to the tightening of regulations. The plan, backed by Rome and by John von Staupitz, Vicar General of the German congregations, was strongly opposed by the Erfurt group to which Luther belonged. Erfurt was a reformed congregation, and they, along with other "Observantine" houses, objected to union with the "Conventuals" for fear of corruption. Luther, zealous for the strict monastic code, was sent to Rome in 1510, along with an older monk from another convent, to make an appeal on behalf of the houses that observed the reformed regulations and opposed the plan of union. The two monks lacked official sanction from Staupitz and were unsuccessful in their mission on behalf of their brothers. But it gave Luther the chance to see the *Eternal City!*

He spent about four weeks in Rome, during which, according to a later reflection, he ran through all the churches and crypts of the city like a crazy saint, anxious to visit all the holy monuments and see the vast array of relics, making the rounds of the gullible pilgrim, taking advantage of the great store of merits waiting for the faithful visitor who would see the Holy City. He found so many opportunities to do things for the poor souls departed from this earthly life that he was sorry his father and mother were still living. He would have gladly rescued them from their sufferings in the hereafter!

While in Rome he crawled up the *Scala Sancta*, the steps that Christ supposedly descended after being sentenced. This act of devotion was said to free a soul from purgatory. Desiring to release his grandfather from punishment, Luther climbed up on his knees, piously kissing each step and praying a *Pater Noster*. When he reached the top, however, he was seized by the same old doubt. "Who knows whether it is true?" he murmured anxiously.

There was much to behold in the religous capital, but not all of it was holy or beautiful. One of the things that most disturbed Luther was the way in which the Italians treated the Mass. The priests seemed concerned only about freeing the altars so they could make their daily quota of Masses. Their haste and irreverence gave them little patience for Luther's celebration. "*Passa, Passa,*" they said to him. "Hurry up, have done with it!" Luther returned home five months later, much more aware of the world in which he was living.

Staupitz' plan of union eventually had to be dropped because of the unyielding opposition. Whether or not Luther's views changed on the issue is not known, but Staupitz recalled him to Wittenberg in 1511 and appointed him preacher to the monks at the Black Cloister. Meanwhile Luther continued his theological studies. By the fall of 1512, Staupitz had arranged for Luther's promotion to the Doctorate and for Luther to take over the Vicar General's own teaching chair in Biblical Studies. He also made Luther subprior of the Wittenberg cloister, a position that gave him responsibility for the instruction of the novitiates.

Presiding over the doctoral ceremonies was Professor Andreas Carlstadt, who later was to become engaged in a bitter controversy with Luther. He placed the doctor's ring on Luther's finger, one of the acts that marked the culmination of Luther's formal academic training. Luther had passed the rigorous requirements, received the necessary approbation, and at the age of twenty-nine was elevated to the position of Doctor of Theology, though in his heart he had not yet experienced the theological breakthrough that was to lead him into spiritual conflict with the papacy.

The first course that he taught in his new position as Doctor of the Holy Scriptures was on the book of Genesis. Then, during the years 1513-1515, he lectured on the Psalms. He quickly established himself as a careful scholar and a forceful teacher, gaining the respect of both students and faculty.

His concern for rightly interpreting the Scriptures led him to seek new knowledge of Greek and Hebrew from his colleague and friend, Johann Lang, and it was through Lang that Luther met George Spalatin—a relationship that was to have far-reaching consequences, for Spalatin soon rose to the position of secretary to Prince Frederick, in whose territory Wittenberg was located, and was to play a key role in gaining political support for Luther's cause of the Gospel.

In addition to his teaching duties, Luther had other equally demanding responsibilities. He began preaching in the Town Church. (He preached over one hundred and seventy sermons in one year!) This, along with his work as subprior of the

Black Cloister, made heavy claims upon his time. He was still required to keep his monastic devotions, and often he found himself on Saturday morning, trying to make up the religious exercises he was unable to keep during the week.

Throughout his lectures on the Psalms, Luther's thought remained preoccupied with the holiness of God and the staggering effect of his Law upon those who took him seriously. For Luther at this time, a broken spirit, initiated by the accusing word of God, was the believer's only righteousness. That is, by confessing his own utter worthlessness, the believer made God right in his word of judgment on sinful humanity (Romans 3:4) and through this self-reproachment escaped eternal damnation. This "theology of humility" left little to rejoice in, and Luther was given over to periods of despondency and restless brooding, though he was kept from complete despair by the wise counsels of Vicar General Staupitz who encouraged Luther in his work and spoke to him words of spiritual consolation. Luther was later to acknowledge on many occasions his great debt to Staupitz. The Reformer attributed to the Vicar General an important role in the awakening of the Gospel in his life.

Discovery of the Gospel of God

In 1515, Staupitz appointed Luther District Vicar of the Augustinians. This gave Luther jurisdiction over eleven cloisters. Also in this year, Luther launched his lectures on Paul's Letter to the Romans, lectures that proved to contain the seeds of new theological insights that were to mature and become the source for a radical reorientation in Luther's life and thought. Strongly under the influence of Augustine, Luther penetrated into the depth dimension of the letter.

A new spirit emerged in him as he looked more and more

to the Scriptures for his religious authority. Wrestling with the Apostle's writing, he became acutely aware of the discrepancy between the truth it revealed and the existing practices of the medieval church–not simply in the church's moral life, but in its theological thought as well. He began stinging attacks upon the clergy. He warned against the mentality that sought religious security in good works. In his sermons, he exposed excesses prevalent in the veneration of saints. He discredited certain legends surrounding the apostles. He declared a work long attributed to St. Augustine to be nonauthentic, an act that brought forth anger from even his own ordinarily sympathetic university colleagues. And he began forceful attacks on the venerated philosopher, Aristotle, calling this champion of the schoolmen a "clown of the university," asserting the incompatibility of philosophical reason with the theology of Scripture. Luther more and more boldly thrust the light of God's word into the darkened life of the church, searching the spiritual depths of man, revealing total corruption and the bondage of the human will to self-interest even at the height of religious concern.

While Luther grew in wisdom and reputation as he labored with the Scriptures, he was still troubled with inner resentment toward the God whom he served. To a sensitive conscience, under emotional stress, certain words or phrases have a way of causing near-panic, conveying a power quite beyond that of ordinary usage, setting off in the receiver terrifying associations, so that the very thought of the word is enough to fill the person with dread. The "justice" or "righteousness" of God was such a term for Luther. And when he encountered the sentence in Romans 1:17, "For in [the gospel] the righteousness of God is revealed," his spirit raged within him. In his words:

> As though it really were not enough that miserable sinners should be eternally damned with original sin and have all kinds of calamities laid upon them by the law of the Ten Commandments, God must go and add sorrow upon sorrow and even through the gospel itself bring his justice and wrath to bear![6]

As he further struggled with this stumbling block, through his linguistic study he came to understand the term "righteousness of God" in the Hebraic sense—not that out of which he damns sinners, but that out of which *he makes sinners righteous*. It was a wholly new way of viewing the concept. God's righteousness was really his mercy! Divine justice, contrary to human understanding, was that which made the unjust just. Luther's "theology of humility" in which man bowed in terror before the menacing holiness of the Lord was but one side of the picture—the negative side. Crushing the sinner with the Law was only one aspect of salvation. This was God's *alien* work. "God must slay before He can raise up," Luther said. But his true and proper work, according to Luther's maturing theology, was his merciful work in Christ: rebuilding the broken and contrite spirit. There was through faith the happy exchange of his righteousness for our sin. Luther expressed it this way in a letter to an Augustinian brother who later became an Evangelical pastor:

> Learn Christ and him crucified; learn to pray to him despairing of yourself, saying: Thou, Lord Jesus, art my righteousness, but I am thy sin; thou hast taken on thyself what thou wast not, and hast given me what I was not. Beware of aspiring to such purity that you will not wish to seem to yourself, or to be, a sinner. For Christ only dwells in sinners. For that reason he descended from heaven, where he dwelt among the righteous, that he might dwell among sinners. Consider that kindness of his, and you will see his sweetest consolation.[7]

And so it was with the other attributes of God—his wisdom, his strength, his glory. God's wisdom was that by which he makes us wise. God's strength was that by which he makes us strong. God's glory was that by which he humbles himself for our sake in Christ. The Divine Attributes were to be viewed as God-in-merciful-relation to sinful man, and not in the old formal, active sense of what God is in himself—Absolutes of Perfection out of which he judges that which is imperfect or seeks that which most compliments his own nature.

Emerging in Luther's vision was a gracious God who "so loved the world that he gave his only Son, that whoever believes in him should not perish but have eternal life" (John 3:16, *RSV*). Faith in Christ replaced abject humility as the source of the believer's righteousness in Luther's theology. With the dawning of this understanding, Luther felt as though the gates of paradise had opened.

The Indulgence Controversy

It was only natural that Luther's new evangelical insights should lead him into conflict with the indulgence traffic of his day. The practice of indulgences had many critics, but it remained for Luther's voice to precipitate the storm. The church taught that a man whose sin was forgiven through confession must still make satisfaction for his sins. While the *guilt* of sin was forgiven, sin had earthly consequences and acts of contrition assigned by the priestly confessor were meant to rectify wrongs and concretely demonstrate the sincerity of the penitent. Indulgences were means by which these temporal penalties could be reduced or waived. There was in heaven a treasury of merits established by the sufferings of Christ and enriched from time to time by the meritorious life of an outstanding saint. From this treasury could be drawn the necessary merits to make satisfaction for sins. For the right price one could be released from the penalties imposed by the church.

What was originally thought to be a pastoral accommodation to the people became an accepted way for the church to raise money, an integral part of its economics, and often in the process misunderstandings arose concerning the nature of indulgences. People were led to believe that they were actually purchasing forgiveness of sin and were hence set free from any penalty that God might impose, when, as Luther argued, indulgences only had the power to release a person from the burdens imposed by the church.

So accepted had the indulgence institution become that Luther never at first really questioned its validity—only the abuse and false understanding which led to the neglect of inner repentance and false security before God. Before he was through, however, he stood opposed to the whole business.

His involvement in the issue came about in this way: the Archbishopric of Mainz had been purchased from Rome by Albert of Brandenburg, a man too young to legally hold the position and who, in violation of church law, already held two other ecclesiastical offices. However, Pope Leo X was willing to overlook these irregularities because of the large sum of money that he had received from Albert and the further promise of gaining even more through the sale of a special jubilee indulgence throughout Albert's territory—a sale that would not only aid the Pope in his plans to complete the lavish St. Peter's Cathedral project in Rome, but would help Albert pay back his debt to the Fuggers, a wealthy German lending house that had financed his purchase of the office. Albert employed the Dominican monk, John Tetzel, as one of his indulgence salesmen. Tetzel came within twenty miles of Wittenberg, hawking the "heavenly insurance policies,"

using the crassest appeals to encourage business and promising benefits which were outright blasphemous—sweeping release from *all* penalties, both heavenly and temporal, even for one's relatives in purgatory. This was too much for Luther. People over whom he had pastoral charge began appearing in the confessional, expecting absolution without sorrow for their sins or any desire to change their lives—all because they possessed Tetzel's jubilee indulgence. When Luther refused to prostitute his priestly office, they returned angrily to Tetzel demanding explanation. Tetzel in turn began attacks on the Wittenberg priest.

It was not until after Luther had obtained a copy of Albert's instructions to his salesmen concerning the indulgence that Luther sought concerted action to meet this menace. The instructions so aroused his indignation that he prepared his *Ninety-Five Theses On the Power and Efficacy of Indulgences*, propositions to be debated by the community of scholars in the hopes that out of this discussion steps might be taken to remedy the shameful practices that were, according to Luther, keeping people from the mercy of Christ and from the spirit of true repentance.

Luther drafted the order of the theses in reference to Albert's booklet of instructions on the indulgence and sent copies to Albert and others directly concerned. On the eve of All Saints Day, October 31, 1517, he posted his Latin disputation on the door of the Castle Church. The city of Wittenberg was crowded with pilgrims who had come for the great religious festival to purchase special indulgences and view the 17,443 relics on display. While Luther's prince, Frederick, had forbidden the sale of Albert's papal indulgence in his territory, Frederick was not averse to the use of relics and indulgences for his own monetary gain. In fact, he was a most eager advocate of this type of approach. Aware of the delicate situation, Luther still felt compelled to direct himself to what he saw to be a spiritually disastrous issue.

In his famous theses for a disputation on indulgences, Luther asserted that the *whole* of the Christian life was to be one of repentance. He expressed concern about the exploitation of the poor who purchased indulgences rather than looking after the needs of their own families. And he opposed the buying of indulgences with money that should be spent in acts of charity toward the sick and disinherited.

Luther proposed that the Pope can by indulgences remit penalties which the Pope has imposed, namely, acts of penance to be performed by the living. But the Pope cannot remit penalties which God has imposed and cannot, therefore, release souls from purgatory. As for the living, Luther said, every Christian who truly repents is forgiven and needs no indulgence.

The *Theses* were never formally debated. They were quickly translated and within the month copies had spread throughout all of Germany. The growing sense of national identity, and the correlative dissatisfaction with the siphoning of money by the Italian papacy, linked itself with Luther's *Theses*, finding in them a kind of "manifesto." Also, the laity, long suffering under the fear of clerical power, sensed in them the direction to a freedom from priestly tyranny.

Albert appealed to his theologians at the University of Mainz for interpretation, but they directed him to put the matter before the Pope. When the subject was first called to Leo's attention, he is reported to have referred to Luther as a drunken German who would think differently when he sobered up. Later, however, he requested the General of the Augustinians in Rome to silence the German monk.

Meanwhile, Luther's enemies began shifting the point of debate from the indulgence abuse to that of the authority of the Pope. Luther was assailed as a heretic. John Eck, a theologian of considerable repute whom Luther considered a friend, published a tract in which he associated Luther's doctrines with those of John Hus, the Bohemian reformer who had burned at the stake for heresy. As the opposition grew, largely through the efforts of Tetzel's Dominican Order, it became clear to Luther and his friends that his own life was in great danger.

The Protest Against Rome

On August 7, 1518, Luther received a summons to appear in Rome. He was given sixty days. Sensing the intrigue that lay behind the papal order, Luther appealed to Prince Frederick, requesting that his trial be held in Germany where he could be sure of safe conduct and a fair hearing; but the Pope had a sudden change of mind about the sixty-day grace period and ordered the immediate arrest of Luther by the papal legate, Cardinal Cajetan.

It was at this point that Luther's friendship with Spalatin, Prince Frederick's court chaplain and a strong admirer and confidant of Luther's really proved itself. Although Luther had attacked indulgences, a subject very close to Frederick's heart, and although the Prince had never met Luther in person, through the influences of Spalatin he was sympathetic to his Wittenberg professor and felt a protective responsibility for him. Refusing to allow Luther to be arrested, he proposed to Cajetan that a fair trial be held in Germany. Cajetan countered with the proposal that he himself hold a conference with Luther, in an atmosphere of friendliness, to determine his standing in the Holy Catholic faith.

When approval for this new plan of dealing with the Luther problem was received from Rome, Luther was called to Augsburg to appear before the Cardinal. Cajetan's fatherly attitude, displayed in the interviews, did not get in the way of his single-minded intention, which was to make Luther recant. He soon found, however, that Luther was remarkably well-schooled, confident in his opinions, and unwilling to accept anything not adequately supported from Scripture.

As the interviews progressed, Cajetan discovered, much to his alarm, that Luther's views were even more threatening than previously thought. Luther had been pushed into doing some painstaking research on the history of the papacy by his enemies who insisted on making the indulgence issue one of papal authority. Out of this study came the slowly unfolding story that the papacy could and, indeed, *had* erred. And further, that church councils also could and *had* erred. By questioning the infallibility of the church in speaking for Christ, Luther was undermining the very foundation of the Roman institution. While Cajetan might have admitted the debatability of the original theses, Luther's new assertions were to him clearly heretical. The Cardinal's fatherly attitude soon gave way to anger and in a fit of temper he ordered Luther out of his presence until the day when he should turn from his errors. Deeply upset by his failure to bring Luther to submission, Cajetan warned Frederick to turn the Wittenberg heretic over to papal authorities or drive him from the land. Frederick, however, remained in favor of a free trial and requested a statement from Rome listing Luther's errors.

Another papal representative, Charles von Miltitz, himself a Saxon, was sent to Germany to "soften-up" Frederick with the coveted papal decoration, "The Golden Rose," hoping thereby to obligate the prince to hand Luther over. Frederick remained unmoved by this gesture, though Miltitz did succeed in arranging a meeting with Luther, at which he promised a trial before a German bishop if Luther would promise to keep silent. Luther agreed to Miltitz' offer providing that his opponents would likewise keep silent. Miltitz, anxious to prove himself an able diplomat, conveyed the arrangement to the Pope, with a falsely optimistic report of Luther's position, giving Rome a wrong reading of the situation. They were ready to welcome the submissive Wittenberg priest back into the bosom of the Holy Mother Church.

The silence was not kept for long, however. Luther considered himself attacked by John Eck, the celebrated debater from the University of Ingolstadt who had been carrying on a controversy with Luther's colleague, Andreas Carlstadt. Eck's arguments were emerging clearly as direct assaults upon Luther's position, and Luther felt compelled to respond. He turned his pen against the Ingolstadt theologian and the silence that Miltitz had hoped for was broken.

A much publicized debate was arranged between Eck and Carlstadt at the University of Leipzig. Luther accompanied his fellow Wittenberg professor in the anticipation that he himself might get the chance to face Eck in the presence of the distinguished audience and receive a fair hearing of his views. He waited for nearly a week while Eck and Carlstadt fought it out. Eck's erudition and his flare for the dramatic, in contrast to Carlstadt's methodical, bookish approach, won for him the unanimous support of the audience. It was then that he sought to topple Luther.

Up until this time, Luther had generally assumed the basic integrity of the Roman Church in which he had been nurtured. He believed that if he could just get a fair hearing, the Pope and the church at large would recognize the truth and take the necessary steps to reform. The reception of his convictions, however, did not correspond with his hopes. Challenged and thrown into battle, he was pressed into further examining some of Rome's most cherished doctrines, and he found them to be the precepts of men.

On July 4, 1519, Luther officially entered the dispute with Eck. The two men argued until July 14, often with heated tempers. Eck immediately employed the "guilt by association" principle, linking Luther directly with the teachings of John Hus. Hus was a symbol of everything bad, and when Luther stated that some of his opinions were sound Catholic teaching, the crowd was appalled. Eck further pushed Luther on the matter of religious authority until Luther was forced to state the fallibility of everything except the revealed Word of God in the Scriptures. On the matter of indulgences, over which all the trouble had originally started, Eck was most conciliatory. Luther later remarked that if he had been answered with the views of Eck on indulgences when he first posted the *Theses*, "the world would have never heard of Martin Luther."

The records of the debate were submitted to the Universities of Erfurt and Paris for a decision as to the winner. Even though the debate was officially over, the real battle was only beginning. Luther and a rapidly growing number of followers vied with Eck and his camp of orthodox Romans, the inevitable break with Rome all the while becoming more and more apparent.

The death of Maximilian, Emperor of the Holy Roman Empire, the mystical political structure that unified the Western world, and the ensuing problems of election, took attention away from the religious revolution that was in the making long enough to permit Luther needed time to develop the ramifications of his evangelical doctrines. He worked prodigiously in this period, preaching, teaching, writing–disseminating his ideas and gathering strength for the war ahead. It was certain that he was not going to let his protest on behalf of the Gospel go unheard. And it was equally certain that Rome would not let his protest go unchecked. By establishing the power of the church in the redemptive action of God in Christ rather than in human righteousness and ecclesiastical organization, it looked as if Luther would have to answer with his life. For as Erasmus said: "Luther committed two sins, namely, he attacked the crown of the Pope and the bellies of the monks."

ENEMIES OF THE GOSPEL

"There is to be freedom of choice in everything that God has not clearly taught in the New Testament, for example, in matters pertaining to various foods, beverages, attire, places, persons and various forms of conduct [Rom. 14:2-6; 1 Cor. 8:8-10]. We are obligated to do nothing at all for God, except believe and love."[8]

The Message of Freedom

Luther's conflict with Rome has often been described by such words as rebellion, revolt, defiance, and other terms that imply headstrong individualism. This does not really do justice to the spirit of Luther's cause. Evangelical Protestantism, of which Luther was the father, was more closely aligned with the root meanings of these words–Evangelical coming from the Greek *euangelion*, meaning "good news," and Protestant coming from the Latin *protestari*, meaning to "bear testimony" or "show forth." The central purpose of Luther and his followers was to proclaim the good news of God concerning his Son, Jesus Christ. The fundamental assertion was the free forgiveness of sin, while we are yet sinful, through faith in Jesus Christ, and the manifestation of this forgiveness in the believer's joyful performance of his many earthly responsibilities, through which he provides useful service to his fellow man.

Luther called for the "dethronement" of man-made laws

which in actual practice had been elevated to the status of divine commandments, making people guilty over things they ought not to be guilty about, and directing them away from the things about which they ought really to be concerned. Whenever religious man is not disciplined by the Gospel, Luther said, he makes laws where there are no laws, elevating preliminary matters to ultimate concerns. Luther recognized the crippling effects these laws had on the spontaneity of life—how, in matters of food, drink, and sex alone, a sensitive conscience could be enslaved by human regulations, so driven by fear and bound by guilt as to result in a severe disease, and never really face his true sins before God, such as unbelief, spiritual pride, despair, and lack of concern for social justice. In addition to the call to end the tyranny of human regulations, Luther asked Rome to concede that even if one were to prove faithfully obedient to the divine commandments themselves, it would not help earn righteousness, obtain mercy, or atone for sin. Only trust in Christ accounted for one's salvation. This was the Evangelical Principle that decried the significance of human and ecclesiastical merit in the process of salvation, and which Luther insisted must be the foundation of the Christian life.

This faith of which Luther spoke was not simple assent to an idea, nor a list of correct teachings to which to adhere, nor even belief in past historical saving events of which the Bible speaks. For Luther, man was not saved by recollection, correct knowledge, or assent to a creed, but through trust in the promises of the living God. Luther liked to use the illustration of a sick man and his physician. While a man in his illness can feel nothing but pain and the ravages of disease and can see nothing but suffering and death in the offing, the doctor assures him with kindly words that he will get well. The man has nothing at the moment to which to appeal for support of this promise by the physician. All the evidence is against it. Yet he clings to this word of hope and is made well in his faith. Such was the nature of saving faith in God. For Luther, it was *confidence-in-spite-of*. Man was made well by trusting God in his Word to him—his Word that pronounced forgiveness, eternal identity, and a meaningful role in his work of redeeming the world, all of which was contradictory to the evidence produced by the Devil in moments of religious struggle.

By 1520 it became clear that the Pope was not going to accept Luther's call for evangelical reform. Luther turned then to the laity. In his *Open Letter to the Christian Nobility of the German Nation*, he assailed the corruption of Rome and appealed to the civil rulers to do something about it. In this reform tract, Luther set forth the important doctrine of the priesthood of all believers. By this doctrine, Luther did not mean to give license to "individualized" religion, though many interpreted him to mean that each Christian, since he was a priest, had direct access to God and was in no need of any intermediary. Luther held that in baptism, each Christian became a priest, that is, to him were entrusted the holy things of God, namely the Gospel of forgiveness and the promise of eternal life. The Christian, in turn, was to be a priest to his fellow man, speaking the promises of Christ and offering divine consolation in his name. Christians, according to Luther, were not their own priests before God, but were *priests to one another*. Because every Christian was a priest, he was to share in responsibility for the welfare of the church. It was on this ground of common priesthood that Luther called the laity to reform action.

A few months later, another tract appeared entitled *The*

Babylonian Captivity of the Church, in which Luther charged that the whole sacramental system of the Roman Church was an insidious scheme by which an ecclesiastical elite held power over all other Christians. He acknowledged the validity of only two of the traditional seven sacraments–Baptism and the Lord's Supper. They were the only two, according to Luther, that met the threefold criterion of being instituted by Christ, of proclaiming the forgiveness of sin, and of using an earthly element (water, bread, wine). All the others failed to meet one or more of these requirements.

While Luther was working day and night to meet the many new challenges that were arising, John Eck was also active.[9] In Rome as chief adviser to the Pope on the Luther problem, Eck succeeded in awakening the Pope to the seriousness of the matter and in implementing the heresy proceedings against the Wittenberg professor. In Luther's words, Eck was the "Pope's Holy Spirit." He helped draft the famous bull, *Arise, O Lord*, in which Luther was given sixty days to recant or suffer the fate of being cut off from God and man. In addition, the bull called for the burning of all Luther's works in order to remove every trace of his heresy. Luther's response to this was to burn those tomes of Canon Law that supported the supremacy of the Pope and to throw the bull itself into the fire at a well-attended ceremony on the outskirts of Wittenberg. The general reaction throughout Germany to the papal declaration was not in Rome's favor. Luther had become a national hero.

One last effort was made by Luther to convince the Pope of the legitimacy of the evangelical protest. Charles von Miltitz, who still had not given up in his efforts to negotiate a settlement between Luther and Rome, persuaded Luther to write something "nice" for the Pope. This Luther did in the treatise, *The Freedom of a Christian.* It was a warm, pastoral exposition, clarifying his position on good works, and elucidating the Christian's freedom from the tyranny of all human regulations and claims upon his conscience, and the equally important obligation of love toward one's fellow man—a twofold concept stated by Luther in the following way:

> A Christian is a perfectly free lord of all, subject to none.
> A Christian is a perfectly dutiful servant of all, subject to all.

The Freedom of a Christian remains to this day one of Luther's most significant writings. He never received a personal response—only the final bull of excommunication which appeared on January 3, 1521.

On Trial Before the World

Charles V of Spain had been elected Emperor of the tottering Holy Roman Empire following the death of his grandfather, Maximilian. After his coronation in Germany, he convened his first diet at Worms. There were several pressing issues, not the least of them the matter of Martin Luther, whose popularity was mounting daily. Even though Rome had pronounced its final anathema against Luther, Charles was restricted by imperial law which forbid that a German be taken outside his own country for trial or that one be banned without a hearing. Against his own better wishes, Charles summoned Luther to Worms to appear before the Diet, offering him safe conduct. Luther traveled to Worms as a celebrity. He was cheered along the way and received numerous invitations to preach. But at Worms, the reception was even more impressive. Trumpets sounded as the party was seen approaching. An escort was sent forth, and the city streets jammed with well-wishing spectators. Luther and his party could hardly make their way to their quarters because of the crowd. It was an exciting prelude to the long-awaited showdown.

The next afternoon, Luther went before the Emperor and the impressive body of ruling dignitaries who composed the German Diet. He was asked if the collection of books on a table near him were his, and if he were ready to retract the heresies they contained. The chancellor of Luther's prince interjected at this point and asked that the titles be read. They were—twenty-five in all. Luther, somewhat dismayed by the whole proceeding, acknowledged that the writings were his, but as for the second part of the question, said that he needed more time before giving an answer. This request was granted, though the Roman officials were furious, including the papal nuncio, Aleander, who for months had been working behind the scenes to bring this chapter in the history of "heresies" to a close.

Luther returned to his room, where throughout the night and the next day he labored over what he was to say. (The notes he prepared for this crucial historic moment are still in existence.) At four o'clock in the afternoon, he was taken to a different assembly hall, larger and more crowded than the one in which he had appeared the day before. He was kept waiting outside until six o'clock. Candles were lighted. Finally Luther was called to give answer.

He was a different man as he addressed the royal assembly on this occasion. He had the composure of one who had made his decision. Come hell itself, nothing could divert him from his stand. He stated that not all of his books fell into the same category. Some parts dealt with simple Christian piety and were worthy of being read by all Christians. Other parts attacked the papacy. To retract them, Luther said, would be to open the door to even greater evils than now existed. Still

MP

other parts were directed against individuals who sought to preserve the Roman tyranny, and while he agreed that in these he had been more violent than his profession demanded, it was not he who was on trial, but the truth of Christ, which he would not retract for fear that the patronage of the papacy continue.

"Will you or will you not recant your errors?" came the impatient question again.

Luther realized the time had come. He spoke out:

> Unless convinced by the testimony of Scripture or right reason—for I trust neither the Pope nor councils inasmuch as they have often erred and contradicted one another—I am bound in conscience, held captive by the Word of God in the Scriptures I have quoted. I neither can nor will recant anything, for it is neither right nor safe to act against conscience. God help me! Amen.

Luther in Hiding

Because of complex political reasons, the Emperor's imperial ban on Luther and his followers was not immediately forthcoming. The Edict of Worms, which called for Luther's arrest and the death of anyone who harbored him or his writings, was proclaimed on May 26, more than a month later; and then only by approval of a rump session of the Diet. By this time, Luther had been spirited away, his whereabouts unknown to the world.

After Luther's courageous stand at Worms, Frederick the Wise had taken immediate steps to protect Luther's life. Aware that only a few days of his safe-conduct pledge remained, Frederick, in a secret plot, arranged for the "capture" of the Wittenberg professor on his way back to the university town. Overtaken in the Thuringian forest in a mock ambush, Luther was carried off to the Wartburg, an ancient castle-fortress near Eisenach. There the theologian was remodeled into a German knight called "Junker George." He was confined to his room until his beard and monk's haircut grew long enough to hide his ordinary likeness, and during this time he was thoroughly trained in the customs of a nobleman.

In the solitude of the Wartburg, the full realization of the magnitude of the events in which he was involved burst upon Luther. He was given over to grave doubts about his course of action. Could it be possible that he himself had been deceived? Who was he, he reasoned uncertainly, to question the tradition of centuries? And what was going to be the fate of all those who had forsaken Rome and joined the evangelical cause? In addition to these second thoughts about his own role in the tumultuous events, he was subject to attacks of inner religious anxiety—severe spiritual agony that he called *Anfechtung*. These were awful moments of temptation when God's presence seemed withdrawn, when he was flooded with the feeling of abandonment and shaken by the threat of chaos and hell. He had learned to know this experience well through the years, though the pain of it never lessened. Luther struggled through these "assaults of the Devil" with intensive work. He continued his voluminous correspondence, wrote devotional materials, sermons, polemical tracts, and perhaps most important of all, translated the entire New Testament into German—a task he accomplished in only eleven weeks.

Back in Wittenberg, Luther's followers rallied to the call he had sounded at Worms. Under the leadership of Andreas Carlstadt, reform attempts were begun. Early in the movement, it became apparent that they might assume explosive proportions. Carlstadt, eager to get on with things, went overboard in his zeal, completely unconcerned with the consciences of those who were still strongly attached to the thought and ceremonies of the Roman Church. He began setting up new regulations, making pronouncements on what had to go and what had to be instituted in matters of worship, ceremonies, and daily living. He urged the monks and nuns to break with their monastic vows and to take for themselves wives and husbands. (He himself married a fifteen-year-old girl.) He celebrated the Holy Communion in his street clothes, inviting the laity to help themselves at the altar to both the bread and the wine. And in his reform zeal, Carlstadt, along with an impassioned Augustinian monk named Zwilling, inspired mobs of local citizens and students to smash idols, images, shrines, and other things that reminded them of Rome.

The first reports that came from Wittenberg apparently were not detailed enough to alarm Luther. He was glad to learn that the cause of the Gospel was not resting idle while he was in seclusion. But word of continued disturbances led him to make a secret visit to Wittenberg in early December of 1521. At this time, he was reassured by his friends that the initial excesses were now under control. Not long after his return to the Wartburg, however, spiritual leaders from Zwickau arrived in Wittenberg, claiming to have immediate access to God and to be inspired with his visions. The Wittenberg camp, including Philip Melanchthon, was impressed by their evident piety and their remarkable command of the Bible from which they could proof-text at will to support their theological peculiarities. The various spiritual aids, helps, and media of grace to which Rome attached so much importance were disparaged by the "heavenly prophets" from Zwickau, who claimed they could talk directly with God. They envisioned a new social order, to be ushered in by righteous force, in which there would be no class distinction, no work that was not manual labor, no formal education (reliance only on heavenly inspiration), no urbanization, and no commercial trade–just simple, agrarian, communistic living. Carlstadt was so taken by their ideas that he suddenly refused to be called "Doctor" any longer and went into the fields to try his hand at physical labor. Things in Wittenberg went from bad to worse, and even the closest friends of Luther were at a loss as to what to do. In early March of 1522, Luther, despite the strong objections of Prince Frederick and in face of the imperial ban, came forth out of hiding to fight the new enemies of the Gospel.

The Protest Against the Radical Reformers

The enthusiasm of the radicals for destruction and their support of the violent overthrow of the old order were outlawed by Luther. He insisted that no physical force be used to bring about the reform, only preaching, teaching, writing, and speaking the Gospel of God. These things they were to engage in vigorously that the Word of God be set forth. But he stood opposed to the use of force to advance the cause of Christ. He cited his own case as an example–how the reformation events had taken hold through the proclamation of the Word. "Philip and I sat drinking beer," Luther said. "The *Word* did the work!" The Word was mightier than any sword, for Luther knew the battle was not against flesh and blood, but against the powers of spiritual darkness.

Luther defended the right of those who had not yet been grasped by the freedom of the Gospel. He maintained that re-education would take time, and that many would have to be weaned slowly from the old ways. He took the middle ground. Where the Roman error was idolatry, the enthusiasts' error was iconoclasm. Luther said that if a statue or an image, music and vestments, or anything else he called adiaphora (incidentals) did not get in the way of the pure doctrine of the mercy of Christ and trust in his forgiveness, then the believer had the right to chose to use them for spiritual support. Anyway, said Luther, the externals were not the issue. The evangelical reformation was a matter of the heart. Luther always remained conscious of the historical development of the church and of being part of that movement of history. He had no desire to reinstitute the practices and customs and organizational procedures of the New Testament church, to jump back over the years as though the evolving life of the church was to be ignored. What Luther wanted to reinstitute was the *Gospel* of the New Testament church, not the polity and practice of that milieu. In this he differed from most of the other reformers who sought to use the New Testament church as a model or prototype.

Upon his return to Wittenberg, Luther wrote an explanation of his action to Prince Frederick, publicly absolving the Prince of all responsibility for his reappearance at this time. He then preached for eight consecutive days, and through forceful evangelical sermons once again resumed command. It was a relief to the whole city to have Luther back, though Carlstadt, his former friend, was soon to leave in disgust at the conservative posture Luther was assuming. The charge of the radicals was that Luther had not gone far enough. He became to them a symbol of the status quo. Some of the radicals claimed to be more biblical than Luther. They cited text after text from both the Old and the New Testaments about idols, images, customs, and church polity to which he was not conforming. In their literalistic use of the Scriptures, they found a whole textbook of standards to which they sought to make the new church conform.

Luther saw in the zealous reform ideas of the fanatic enthusiasts a new threat to the Gospel and to the freedom of a Christian. They were making laws where there were no laws. They were guilty of the same error Rome had been guilty of. Luther was quick to see that it was "the same old monkery with just a different mask." The Gospel, Luther maintained, created *freedom* and *love*, not another set of human do's and don't's. As he said of the radical movement:

> The whole thing is nonsense. Christ himself came upon the errors of scribes and Pharisees among the Jewish people, but he did not on that account reject everything they had and thought (Matt. 23[:3]). We on our part confess that there is much that is Christian and good under the papacy; indeed everything that is Christian and good is to be found there and has come to us from this source.[10]

While Luther was not always so kindly disposed toward the Roman Church, it is clear that he stood well within the mainstream of historical Christianity, and was compelled to spend as much effort setting forth the Gospel in the direction of the "new Protestants" as he was in the direction of Rome.

GROWING PAINS

"I beg that my name may be passed over in silence, and that men will call themselves not Lutheran but Christian. What is Luther? My teaching is not mine. I have been crucified for nobody . . . Let us root out party names and call ourselves Christians, for it is Christ's Gospel we have."[11]

Social and Political Unrest

The years after Worms were characterized by increasing political and social tension. Revolution was in the air. In 1522, at the Diet of Nürnberg, renewed efforts were made by representatives of Adrian IV, the new Pope, to enforce the ban against Luther. Fearful of provoking a civil war, the princes refused to reaffirm the imperial ban, and instead appealed for a general council to settle the matter. In the confusion of the times, Luther's evangelical cause was given temporary freedom from external harassment.

Two events during these years dealt a severe blow to Luther's national prestige. The knights, whose importance in the political structure had declined, entered into war with the great princes of the land in an attempt to regain lost power. Many of the knights used the Gospel reform as a cover-up for their own self-aggrandizement. Luther raised his voice against their methods, condemning even those who had stood by him at the time of Worms. His opposition to their efforts was not looked upon with favor by the knights, who found themselves unable to win against the stronger princes.

Further trouble came with the increasing dissatisfaction of the peasants who had long been sadly oppressed by the ruling classes. Incited by the teachings of Carlstadt and Thomas Muentzer, a leader of the revolutionary reformers, they found in the "new message" inspiration for revolt. The seething resentment swelled until, in 1525, the peasants were storming the countryside, plundering and killing in the name of the new gospel of liberty. Outraged by their riotous insurrection against all established authority and their raising of havoc across the land, Luther lashed out against them, urging the princes to slay the murdering hordes. In his bitter opposition to the Peasants' War, Luther was looked upon as a traitor to the cause of the oppressed.

Luther believed, as did the Apostle Paul (Romans 13), that civil authority was ordained of God for the keeping of order and peace. While he openly deplored the injustices to the poor and others in his time, he could not justify the overthrow of the social-political structure. Christians were to pray, preach, and work for good rulers, but if there was injustice, they were to bear their cross patiently. The fault was not in the offices of authority, but in the ungodly, irresponsible persons who filled the offices. God himself would see to their punishment.

The Two Kingdoms

Basic to Luther's thinking was the doctrine of the Two Kingdoms—the kingdom of Christ and the kingdom of the world, *both* of which were instituted by God for the welfare and happiness of mankind. "God Himself has ordained and established this secular realm and its distinctions, and by His Word He has confirmed and commended them. For without them this life we could not endure."[12]

The secular kingdom was the keeper of a "fallen" humanity. It was governed by the sword and served as a check against the wantonness of sin. It was ordered in such a way that sinful men would be of mutual service to one another, in spite of the inclination to be something other, through the fulfillment of their worldly callings. It was run by natural laws and human regulations—ordinances that were backed up by the threat of physical punishment if one failed to comply. On the other hand, the kingdom of Christ, which had broken into the worldly domain, was concerned first of all with ultimate reality. It was redemptive in character, and its rule was entirely different from that of the secular dimension of existence. In the kingdom of Jesus Christ, the forgiveness of sin reigned, and the teachings of Jesus, such as those found in the Sermon on the Mount, were the norms for behavior. As Luther said:

> In short, the rule in the kingdom of Christ is the toleration of everything, forgiveness, and the recompense of evil with good. On the other hand, in the realm of the emperor, there should be no tolerance shown toward any injustice, but rather a defense against wrong and a punishment of it, and an effort to defend and maintain the right, according to what each one's office or station may require.[13]

The believer, according to Luther, existed in both kingdoms *simultaneously*. He was, in a sense, two persons—at once a Christian man and a citizen of this world. The believer had to learn to distinguish between these two dimensions of his existence, to live with them in *creative tension*, so that, involved in life in this broken world, his actions might be appropriate for the occasion. For example, it might be wrong for a judge to act by the Gospel while serving in the capacity of a civil judge. There he must let the law reign, though in his personal life, in his non-official relations with his fellow man, he is called upon to forgive "seventy-times seven" and to act in accordance with the spirit of the Gospel. For Luther, there was no distinction in the status of people in the kingdom of Christ. All men were equal before God. In the civil realm, however, there were distinctions in rank, power, importance, social worth, wealth, goodness, and other things. These inequalities were to be accepted. The values peculiar to each kingdom were not to be confused with one another.

Because God had instituted both kingdoms, redemption, for Luther, was not an escape from the secular world into some sacred sphere. It was freedom from sin, the fear of death, the power of the Devil, and the threat of hell, in order that one might more freely perform the duties imposed by his calling in the secular world, and also those duties incumbent upon him in his personal life as a Christian. There had always been that heresy which regarded the world as essentially evil, something from which religious man had to be delivered. While Luther recognized that the world was in a fallen state, plagued by evils and imperfections of all sorts, that did not make it *essentially* evil. The God he met in Jesus Christ was not only the Redeemer, but also the Creator who had made the world and all therein. It was still God's creation, and he understood the Gospel as that which renewed man inwardly for outward service in the civil realm. The gospel of forgiveness set one free to love his neighbor as *neighbor* and not as an instrument of salvation.

The Christian, then, was not to seek freedom from secularization. He was to be the *more secular* precisely because he was a Christian! God had given man the commission to care for the earth. Participating in ultimate reality and eternal life *now* through the advent of the kingdom of Christ, the believer was enabled to perform his worldly responsibilities without complaint, greed, laziness, anxiety, rage, lust, dishonesty, and other sins to which one was enslaved before the Gospel. Worldly calling, for Luther, always demanded self-sacrifice. Man did not need to go looking for a cross. It was built into his vocation, if faithfully performed, for man's stations in life were so ordered as to demand the giving up of his person even though one cared nothing for one's neighbor. For example, the unbeliever, in his desire to obtain certain things for himself, was driven to maintain some station in life, and hence, even in his reluctance to serve his fellow man, served the common good through the work he performed. Thus Luther could declare the secular life of man as the proper sphere for good works and bless the faithful performance of one's earthly responsibilities with the Word of God. He also could oppose those who advocated the overthrow of these social orders, which had been ordained by God for the welfare of men.

New Life in the Converted Cloister

In June of 1525, with all of Germany in turmoil over the Peasant Revolt, Martin Luther married Katherine von Bora. Staupitz had released Luther from his monastic vows seven years earlier. The marriage of priests, monks, and nuns had become commonplace with the spread of the Gospel. Many had urged Luther to follow his own teachings, to set an example and take a wife, but Luther, still under the threat of death as a heretic, would have none of it. Therefore, it came as a great surprise to the many who knew him, even such a close colleague as Melanchthon, when Luther announced to the world that in a quiet ceremony he had taken Katherine von Bora to be his wife. Melanchthon was deeply upset that,

just at a time when so many were in distress and in need of Luther's judgment and authority, he sought to occupy himself with marital affairs. He consoled himself with the thought that the marriage might soften Luther's increasing irrascibility and vehemence in polemic (what Melanchthon referred to as "low buffoonery") which were straining the harmony of the evangelical cause.

Katherine was one of nine nuns who had come to Wittenberg two years earlier, having escaped from their convent and fled into Saxony after coming under the influence of Luther's teachings. They were really destitute, without support of family or friends, and they appealed to Luther for help. Luther, who had taken over the Augustinian monastery, gave them temporary shelter until he found housing for them with townspeople. Some of the girls were soon placed as governesses, and some married. After two years, however, Katherine was still around. She had fallen in love with a former Wittenberg student, but his family opposed their marriage and Katherine was left with a sad heart. Luther tried hard to arrange other husbands for her, but she, being of noble birth and proud mind (Luther thought her a bit too proud at times!), was hard to please. Finally it became apparent that it was Luther himself that she desired. At a private ceremony, attended by painter Lucas Cranach and his wife, Luther's close friend Justus Jonas, a university professor of law named Apel, and the town pastor who officiated, John Bugenhagen, Luther and Katherine were married. Luther was forty-two years old; Katherine was twenty-four. The following week a public reception was held.

Years later Luther remarked that had he been of the mind for marriage when the "wagon of vestal virgins" first arrived at Wittenberg, he would have desired Ave Shoenfeld. Of his

Katherine, he said, "I esteem my wife." This initial "respect" deepened as the years evolved into a loving confidence and joy in one another's affections, the spirit of which is captured in the following words of Luther:

> When a man and a woman love and are pleased with each other, and thoroughly believe in their love, who teaches them how they are to behave, what they are to do, leave undone, say, not say, think? Confidence alone teaches them all this . . . Each is a free companion of the other.[14]

They had six children, and in their twenty years of life together, Luther discovered the full truth of the old proverb that he had been taught years before by Frau Cotta: "There is no greater gift on earth than a woman's gift of love to her husband."

Being Luther's wife was not an easy job. The forty-room cloister in which they resided was more like a hotel than an ordinary home. It was the center of Luther's reformation activities. He held his lectures there, entertained guests with food, drink, and conversation, received and housed evangelical refugees, labored at his writings, and generally carried on the work of a world figure. Relatives, students, and friends took up residence and were considered part of the Luther family. The task of maintaining things was immense. Katherine proved herself a woman of remarkable capabilities. She organized the giant household and managed its affairs with all the competence of a skilled business person. The new life in the old cloister bore little resemblance to that which Luther first experienced when he had come to Wittenberg as a young teaching monk some years before. It was obvious that he (who in the fervor of his labors as a celibate at one time had not changed his bedsheets for nearly a year) had found a welcome and able helpmate.

The Emerging Church

The upheavals of the times brought pressure to bear upon Charles V for another German diet, which he called at Spires in 1526. There the princes who were sympathetic to the evangelical cause, managed to lobby for a compromise on the Edict of Worms. According to this compromise, each ruler was to conduct himself in such a way as to be able to defend his position before God and the emperor.[15] This left the religious issue up to the conscience of each ruler. Elector John of Saxony, who had taken rule upon the death of his brother, Frederick the Wise, was even more favorable to Luther and the evangelicals than had been Frederick. His rule permitted the reformers to call upon him directly for support in organizing the emerging church.

The two most immediate problems facing them were the financial and spiritual poverty of the evangelical churches. Monasteries and church properties, which formerly had contributed largely to the support of the work of the church, had been confiscated by the rulers. And the laity, interpreting the gospel of liberty as license, refused to contribute money voluntarily. They were lax in matters of worship, and they neglected their education. The clergy, for the most part, were untrained in the new theology, and many were incompetent by any standards.

At Luther's urging, a commission was established and a plan arranged for the visitation of local parishes to ascertain conditions. Luther prepared a detailed set of instructions for the parish visitors, who would examine both the economic and religious conditions. The findings of the parish visitors were even more staggering than had been imagined. There was widespread excessive drunkenness, "wild-wedlock," gambling, and doctrinal stupidity. Many had outwardly shifted allegiance

XXXXIII

Richte mich herr und füre myr meyne sache. und
der das unheylige volck
und errette mich von den falschen und bösen leuten
Denn du bist der gott meyner stercke. warumb verstössestu mich
warumb lessestu mich so trawrig gehen wenn mich meyn feynd drenget
Sende deyn liecht und deyne warheyt das sie mich leyten
und bringen zu deynem heyligen berge und zu deyner wo
Das ich hyneyn gehe zum altar gottes. zu dem gott der meyne
freuden und wonne, und dyr gott auff der harffen dancke
Gott meyn gott
Was betrübestu dich meyne seele und bist so unrugig ynn myr
harre auff gott. denn ich werde yhm noch dancken das das
heyl seynes angesichts

XXXXV

Eyn unterweysung der kinder Korah vorzusingen.

Gott wyr haben mit unsern oren gehört. unser veter
habens uns erzelet, was du than hast zu yhren zey
ten vor alters
Du hast mit deyner hand die heyden vertrieben und sie eyngesetzt
gepflantzet
du hast die volcker verderbet und sie verstrewet
Denn sie haben das land nicht eyngenomen durch yhr schwerd
und yhr arm halff yhn nicht
sondern deyne rechte, deyn arm und das liecht deynes angesichts
denn du hattest wolgefallen an yhnen
Du bist meyn könig gott
Jacob zu helffen
ir du hilff verheyssest

from Rome to Luther for the sake of their own self-interest, while remaining totally ignorant of Luther's teaching. Emergency preachers had to be substituted in the most outrageous cases, some parishes yoked with one another, and sundry other temporary measures taken to meet the appalling state of affairs, until a new generation of clergy could be trained.

There was urgent need for educational aids to lead the clergy and laity into an understanding of the evangelical faith. Luther sought to fill this gap by preparing an increasing number of sermons that the inexperienced preachers could read to the congregations or use as source material for their own preaching. He also prepared a Catechism—that body of theological knowledge he felt essential to the Christian life. Luther produced many hymns and prayers as well. And finally, one of the greatest contributions was Luther's German translation of the Bible. Begun at the Wartburg, the translation of the Bible was to occupy Luther for the whole of his life. The New Testament appeared in 1522. The first complete edition of the entire Bible appeared in 1534, but continued corrections and improvements were made right up until the year of his death. Weekly, he assembled what he called his "Sanhedrin," composed of the best men available to him, and for several hours before supper at Luther's home they discussed and shared ideas in an effort to get the real meaning of difficult texts and the most accurate translation. Luther said he found the German into which he turned the Greek and Hebrew texts by "looking into the mouth of the man on the street." This very readable translation was of inestimable value to the emerging church whose life was created by the Word of God, Jesus Christ, to whom the Scriptures witnessed.

Luther's profound reverence for the Scriptures, and the

central place that he gave to them in the life of the church, is not to be confused with the jot-and-tittle mentality of later Protestant orthodoxy, which has been accused of instituting a "paper-pope." Luther could call a biblical book, such as the Letter of James, "an epistle of straw" (though he often liked to quote from it), express bafflement at the many contradictions within the biblical corpus, insist on the importance of some biblical material over other biblical material, and in other ways treat the sacred writings with a freedom totally lacking in the slavish bibliolatry of the following generations. In the Book of Jonah, for example, Jonah gives utterance to a beautiful psalm of deliverance while still in the belly of the giant fish. Luther, in commenting on this, said that the psalm must have been composed at some other time, since he doubted that Jonah would have been able to wax that poetic under such unusual circumstances! The difference between Luther's spirit in relation to the Scriptures and that of the orthodoxy that was to follow was that *Luther did not have faith in the Bible*. He had faith in the living Word of God, Jesus Christ (John 1:1), and in the Word of God which is testimony to him, whether in the Scriptures or elsewhere. For Luther, the whole Bible was a book about Christ. (He called it the "swaddling clothes of Christ.") That was what gave it its authority. It was basic to the Christian life because it told of God's Word. This was Luther's "key" to understanding the Scriptures, and through this evangelical principle of interpretation, he found unity amid the diversity of the Old and New Testament voices, and was able to allow and to live with the fact that God himself had not written every comma and period.

DICTATOR OR PROPHET?

"All we aim for is that the glory of God be preserved and that the righteousness of faith remain pure and sound. Once this has been established, namely that God alone justifies us solely by His grace through Christ, we are willing not only to bear the pope aloft with our hands but also to kiss his feet."[16]

Voices of Dissent

Melanchthon's hope that Luther's marriage would modify the reformer's vitriolic polemic was not to come to fruition. If anything, Luther's abusive language against those who disagreed with him increased. While it should be understood that his opponents were not without their own verbal weaponry, Luther's force of soul brought forth expletives that embarrassed even his own followers and made the efforts for unity more difficult.

Luther defended his irascible stubbornness as being the prerogative of his office. He claimed that, as a biblical theologian guarding the truth, the more adamant he could be on matters of faith, the better. In his personal life, however, Luther said he would let love reign. There is evidence that he made this distinction. His public enemy, Andreas Carlstadt, who had done great damage to the evangelical cause, reappeared at Wittenberg in his flight from religious persecution. Despite the bitter public quarrel that Luther had with Carlstadt, he had compassion on the hapless refugee and took him into his household.

In the early years of Luther's protest against Rome, he received widespread support. The whole of Christendom seemed to groan for reform. But as the issues became clearer, he encountered differing opinions and open opposition, all of which he seemed unwilling to tolerate. He was absolutely convinced of the rightness of his doctrine and turned his pen against both friend and foe. This won for him the nickname, "The Pope of Wittenberg."

One of the many he offended was the great humanist scholar, Desiderius Erasmus of Rotterdam. Erasmus, influential in almost every corner of the Empire, worked behind the scenes for Luther's support in the early years. Luther had great respect for his scholarly skills (he had Erasmus to thank for the fine Greek text of the New Testament on which Luther based his own translation), but he had little respect for Erasmus as a theologian and biblical commentator. When Erasmus published *The Freedom of the Will*, in which he asserted that man by acts of willpower can make choices that help achieve righteousness before God, he was attacking the very heart of the evangelical faith. Luther exclaimed that Erasmus had "seized him by the throat," and he countered with a publication entitled *The Bondage of the Will*.

Luther admitted that in the secular kingdom, man had certain choices and could achieve civic and social righteousness. In fact, Luther said, man was to be encouraged in the secular kingdom to justify himself by works. But in his life before God, his reason and his will were impotent. Only God's revelation in Jesus Christ brought man into God's presence and accounted for man's acceptance. Erasmus, in reply to Luther, said,

> It terribly pains me, as it does all good men, that your arrogant, insolent, rebellious nature has set the world in arms . . . as if it were your chief aim to prevent the tempest from ever becoming calm. . . . I should wish you a better disposition were you not so marvelously satisfied with the one you have. . . .[17]

The Sacrament Controversy

Luther's battle with the non-Lutheran evangelicals in southern Germany and Switzerland had even more far-reaching consequences for the unity of the church than did his feud with Erasmus. This controversy was over the nature of the Lord's Supper. Luther had already addressed himself to this subject in his conflict with Rome and in his fight with the radical Carlstadt. The Roman view regarded the sacrament as a sacrifice to God. Carlstadt's view regarded it as a devotional reminder of the suffering and death of Jesus Christ. In both of these views man was the principal actor. Luther rejected them.

Ulrich Zwingli, the Swiss theologian and leading spokesman for the non-Lutheran evangelicals at this time, viewed the sacrament as a confessional recital—the thankful celebration of the objective, historical saving event of God in Christ. In this view, the sacrament was still essentially a work of man—man giving thanks for the Gospel he had received. Luther opposed the Zwinglian position. To him, the Supper was more than a commemorative service. Luther maintained that the sacrament itself was divine grace *in action.* The Lord's Supper was itself a proclamation of the Gospel, God's offer of nothing less than the incarnate Christ himself. The living Lord, who was the Gospel, was present through his Word and Spirit in the broken bread and poured-out wine for the forgiveness of sin, and in faith the believer had union with him.

The matter of the "real presence" of Christ in the sacrament was what the debate was all about when delegates from Switzerland, Strassbourg, and Wittenberg, met at the Marburg Castle in 1529 for their colloquy. A united political front was imperative for the safety of the Protestant territories, and it was hoped that this meeting would solve doctrinal differences and lead to political solidarity. The reformers agreed on fourteen points, but on the Lord's Supper, they stood divided.

Luther insisted on what he called the simple, literal interpretation of the text, "This is my body," the words of Jesus that instituted the sacrament. On the table in the place of meeting, Luther wrote them in Latin–HOC EST CORPUS MEUM–and at a crucial moment in the final stormy session with the Zwinglians he unveiled the words, claiming that upon no other would he take his stand. Just as at Worms, Luther, in the sacrament controversy, was again to take a stand that had great historic consequences. He was convinced that nothing less than the Gospel was at stake.

This final rejection of Zwingli and the non-Lutheran evangelicals left Zwingli in tears. He pleaded on behalf of the peace and unity of the church, saying that there was nothing he and his colleagues wanted more than to be friends with the Wittenberg theologians and to be accepted as brothers in Christ. Luther, however, would have none of it. The two groups parted, with the feeble agreement of mutual toleration.

New Negotiations for Unity

The next major attempt for union came at the Diet of Augsburg the following year, 1530. Each religious body was called upon to prepare a statement of faith, defining their convictions, in the hope that differences could be overcome and a reconciliation with Rome effected. The German estates and princes who had defected from the faith of Rome were now being questioned as to whether or not they had any further right to rule. The Lutherans drafted the famous Augsburg Confession, which, from the political point of view, was the defense of the German leaders for their right to reform the churches within their own area. Heading the Lutheran party was Philip Melanchthon. Luther, a religious outlaw still under the threat of the ban, was forced to remain at the Coburg Castle, miles away from the historic meeting. He who had stood alone before the Emperor at Worms in defense of the Gospel had now become an onlooker and adviser while others took up the cause. Augsburg failed to solve the problem of the dissolution of the Roman political and ecclesiastical synthesis. Germany divided into Catholic and Protestant camps, with the threat of war imminent.

Though the Diet of Augsburg did not accomplish its purpose, it did pave the way for renewed negotiations between the Lutheran and non-Lutheran evangelicals. Martin Bucer of Strassbourg, who had been with Zwingli at the Marburg Colloquy, went to great pains to win the friendship of Melanchthon during the Augsburg proceedings. Bucer succeeded in convincing Melanchthon, and later, Luther, of the sincerity of his purpose, and after much delicate work, the Strassbourg theologian managed to establish an agreement with the Wittenberg party. The report of these discussions, *The Wittenberg Concord*, did not unite the Reformed and the Lutherans, but it made for a new spirit of harmony.

The Old Man at Wittenberg

Luther was not without reason for his skeptical attitude toward the other reform groups. He was particularly sensitive

to the tendency of man to relegate the Gospel to the "use-level" of reality, as though it were something that one could apply to support one's self-interest or to achieve fulfillment of one's personal needs. He had seen the Roman Church, the German knights, the radical reformers, the peasants try to *use* the Gospel for their own ends. He cried out against this, remaining on the alert lest the same spirit work its way into the Lutheran camp.

The Gospel, for Luther, was on the "is-level" of reality. Just as God had identified himself as subject, "I AM WHO I AM," (Exodus 3:14, *RSV*), so too the Gospel "was what it was." Before it, all human claim was silenced. The Gospel defined the reality, the goals, the life, and not, as many would have it, the other way around, as though it were something that could be objectified and used in the attainment of other ends. For example, it was not something one could *use* to

keep the family together, to get peace of mind, or to strengthen declining public morality. Man could not use the Gospel to get discipline. He stood disciplined by the Gospel. Man could not use the Gospel to obtain salvation. The Gospel was salvation. Man did not "get" religion. Religion grasped him. The Gospel, according to Luther, gave man to God. It did not give God to man as though man could then apply God or his Word to solve certain problems or attain his own goals, however virtuous those goals may have been. Luther's "get tough" policy with other reform voices must be understood in light of this if his later years at Wittenberg are to be rightly appreciated.

Even though he had to take a back seat on ecumenical relations, allowing Melanchthon and others to front the Lutheran cause, Luther was by no means idle. He continued preaching and writing, carried on his responsibilities as university professor, counseled those in spiritual distress, and in other ways faithfully performed the duties of pastor-teacher-reformer. He was plagued by severe kidney stone attacks in his mature years and by an inner ear disease, as well as by numerous other aches and pains. He poured out his complaints to his family and friends, and would probably be called a hypochondriac by contemporary standards. Needless to say, these afflictions did not help his already easily irritated temper.

Luther was full of personal incongruities, something especially apparent in his maturing years. He could roar at his enemies with stormy violence, and yet at the same time write charming and tender letters to his wife and children. While he was given to explosive outbursts of anger over theological differences, he maintained, as his recorded *Table Talk* with family and friends indicates, a healthy sense of humor and a spirit of congeniality. While he suffered and complained regularly about so many of his own ills, he wrote moving letters of spiritual consolation to the afflicted and depressed. The contradictions that went into Luther's makeup are nowhere more apparent than in his theologizing itself. As one slightly offended contemporary Roman Catholic scholar has noted about Luther's writings, "sacred things are touched with profane hands and we find a turgid mixture of lofty religious sentiments and thoroughly coarse imagery."[18] Luther could talk of God in barroom language. He could also write and speak of God with an eloquence of style equal to the best of religious poets. In all of this seemingly contradictory behavior, however, it must be said that whatever Luther did, he did it in earnest. He did not play games with people or with theology. He *meant* it. And he had little patience with people who did not *mean* it. He liked to tell the story about how St. Augustine had been asked by someone where God was before heaven was created. Augustine had replied that God was in himself. Luther said that when the same question was put to him, he replied, "God was creating Hell for such idle, presumptuous fools such as you!" Luther maintained that without the Devil's help, everyone would remain a speculative theologian. But because of pain and affliction, sorrow and temptation, man was driven into "meaning it" when he cried to the Lord. The only proper school for Christian theology was the school of hard knocks.

In addition to the physical ills that plagued him in his later years and his increasing discouragement from the way the reformation events were working themselves out, Luther was also to know the humiliation of making a costly mistake in spiritual counsel. As a pastoral accommodation to relieve the supposedly tortured conscience of Landgrave Philip of Hesse, Luther assented to Philip's bigamy, the stipulation being that the second marriage would be kept secret from the public. Philip's first wife did not please him. He had been having affairs with other women and told Luther that his immorality deeply troubled him, stating that the only realistic solution in his weakness would be to take a second wife. Luther, as his pastoral adviser, considering the extenuating circumstances, assented to Philip's plan. So did Philip's first wife. Later, the whole matter became public knowledge. Since bigamy was a crime under imperial law, the Protestant Philip was forced to make great political concessions to the Emperor, concessions that led to the weakening of the Protestant alliance and an eventual defeat from which Protestantism never fully recovered.

The reformer had another major setback in his last years—the death of his fourteen-year-old daughter, Magdelena. She had been Luther's favorite child, and her early death cast Luther into deep sorrow. Adding to his troubles was his increasing disenchantment with Wittenberg. He was bitterly disillusioned by the city's lack of reverence, its ingratitude for the Gospel, and the low standard of public morality it displayed before the world. On more than one occasion, he threatened to leave the city and take up residence elsewhere. During these many periods of discouragement, about the only companion Luther could tolerate (and the only one who could tolerate Luther) was the painter Lucas Cranach. Luther had always found special solace in Lucas' friendship.

Because of his colossal complaints, there is one school of thought that thinks it would have been better if Luther had been martyred at the height of his career and spared the souring years following his charismatic role in the history of the church. This superficial evaluation of Luther's life fails to do justice to his ongoing work as a pastor and teacher, and the continued clarification of his evangelical doctrines. His understanding of the Gospel deepened right up to the end of his life. It used to amaze him that his students thought they so readily understood the evangelical faith, when he himself as an old man was still learning in the school of Christ and the forgiveness of sins.

Many people thought that Luther was a prophet. Though he himself never claimed to be one, he was certain of one thing: that his call and mission came from God. The legacy he left to the church through his productive career is rich and varied, and we are particularly indebted to him for his recovery and clarification of the following doctrines: 1) the sole authority of the living Word, Jesus Christ, who speaks through the scriptures of the Old and New Testaments; 2) our acceptance before God through trust in Christ alone;

3) the right and duty of each Christian to be a priest to his fellow men; 4) the doctrine of vocation or calling as the sphere for good works; and 5) the doctrine of the church as the people of God. The church, for Luther, meant not a building, a visible institution, or an ecclesiastical hierarchy. The church was the people. The marks of the church were not its ecclesiastical continuity, not its ceremonial continuity, not even the holiness of its members. The mark of the church was the right preaching and sacramental celebration of the Gospel of Christ. For wherever the Gospel was preached and the visible proclamation of the Word rightly celebrated, there would be believers. The church was not a static concept for Luther. *The church was happening!* It was people hearing the Gospel—a fellowship being created by the forgiveness of sins through the living Word, Jesus Christ. And it was in the service of this church that Martin Luther spent his life—a life rooted and grounded in the redemptive love of God.

SOLI DEO GLORIA

NOTES

[1] Martin Luther, "Eight Sermons at Wittenberg," *Luther's Works* (55 vols.; Philadelphia: Fortress Press and St. Louis: Concordia Publishing House, 1955-), 51, 70. [Hereafter referred to as *LW*.]

[2] Jonas was an intimate friend of Luther, former Wittenberg professor, and pastor at Halle. Coelius was won over to Luther after the Leipzig Debate, and later became chaplain to Count Albert of Mansfeld.

[3] Gerhard Ritter, *Martin Luther: His Life and Work,* trans. John Riches (New York: Harper and Row, 1963), p. 38.

[4] A. C. McGiffert, *Martin Luther: The Man and His Work* (New York: The Century Co., 1911), p. 8.

[5] Luther, "Heidelberg Disputation," *LW* 31, 57.

[6] Quoted in Wilhelm Pauck (ed. and trans.), *Luther: Lectures on Romans* ("Library of Christian Classics, vol. 15 [Philadelphia: Westminster Press, 1961]), p. xxxvii. For Luther's own expanded account of the matter, see his "Preface to the Complete Edition of Luther's Latin Writings," *LW* 34, 327.

[7] Luther to George Spenlein at Memmingen, *Luther's Correspondence and Other Contemporary Letters,* trans. and ed. Preserved Smith (Philadelphia: Lutheran Publication Society), I, 33.

[8] Luther, "Against the Heavenly Prophets," *LW* 40, 127.

[9] The winner of the Leipzig Debate was never officially declared. Erfurt University refused to give a verdict, and when Paris responded two years later it did so after an evaluation of *several* of Luther's works, which were found to be heretical.

[10] Luther, "Concerning Rebaptism," *LW* 40, 231.

[11] McGiffert, *op. cit.*, p. 215.

[12] Luther, "Sermon on the Mount," *LW* 21, 109.

[13] *Ibid.*, p. 113.

[14] Luther, "A Treatise on Good Works," *Works of Martin Luther*, ed. H. E. Jacobs (6 vols.; Philadelphia: Muhlenberg, 1943), I, 191.

[15] The Augsburg Confession of 1530 was just such a defense on the part of the Lutheran rulers.

[16] Luther, "Lectures on Galatians," *LW* 26, 99.

[17] E. G. Schwiebert, *Luther and His Times* (St. Louis: Concordia Publishing House, 1950), p. 694.

[18] Joseph Lortz, *The Reformation: A Problem for Today*, trans. J. C. Dwyer, S.J. (Westminster, Maryland: Newman Press, 1964), p. 141.